Greek Mythology

A Complete Guide to Greek Mythology,
Greek Gods, and Ancient Greece

Andrew Walsh

Table of Contents

Introduction 1

Chapter 1: How Was the World Created? 3

Chapter 2: Greek Gods and Goddesses 18

Chapter 3: Demi-Gods 35

Chapter 4: Heroes in Greek Mythology 49

Chapter 5: Monsters in Greek Mythology 63

Chapter 6: Famous Greek Mythology Tales 79

Conclusion 89

Introduction

Thank you for choosing this book, detailing the incredible stories of ancient Greek mythology!

If you want to enter the world of Greek mythology and to learn about its heroes and villains, this book has all of it in store for you! This book will cover a wide variety of the famous mythological tales of Greek origin. Whether you want to know about the birth of the Titans or how Medusa became a monster, you will find it all here. If monstrous perils, heart-stirring adventures, and vengeful and scheming gods are something you are interested in, then this book will definitely appeal to your taste. You will also discover stories detailing acts of real bravery and also cowardice, Gods making selfless sacrifices and, on the other hand, committing brutal murders.

By the time you reach the last chapter of this book, you will not only have a general idea of Greek mythology but also have a great appreciation towards it. The twelve main gods of Greek mythology are Zeus, Hephaestus, Hera, Artemis, Apollo, Athena, Hestia, Aphrodite, Ares, Demeter, Hermes, and Poseidon. They are collectively known as the "Olympians" mainly because they are said to live on Mount Olympus. Throughout this book, you will find mention of all these gods, plus many other demi-gods, monsters, and mere mortals in a variety of stories!

Thanks again for taking the time to read this book. Every effort was made to ensure it is full of as much useful and accurate information as possible, so please enjoy!

Chapter 1: How Was the World Created?

Cultures all over the globe have different tales about the creation of the world. Various scholars, especially ethnologists, as well as anthropologists, refer to such stories as 'origin stories' or 'creation myths.' Some of these stories of origin are created based on real events and people, whereas many are simply based on imaginative accounts.

Here, we will cover the creation of the world as it is told in Greek mythology. There are several ancient literary sources detailing this origin story. One of the earliest literary sources is Hesiod's 'The Theogony and Works and Days'. It is believed that the above-mentioned oral poet was active between 750 BCE and 650 BCE. It was during that period when the renowned epics of Homer, namely 'The Odyssey' and 'The Iliad,' took their form. Many authentic archaeological findings have supported the creation story mentioned in Hesiod's work. Some gods and goddesses described by Hesiod are found in various forms of pottery from the 8th century BCE. Before Hesiod told his version of the world's creation through literary means, it was known to everybody in the ancient Greek society orally.

Everything Started with Chaos

According to many Greek cosmologies, the origin of the world began with Chaos. Chaos was known to be the universe's basic feature, and interestingly, was also personified as female. In Greek mythology's origin story, the first beings were born from Chaos.

Story of Uranus and Gaia

At the dawn of the world's creation, the goddess of the Earth, named Gaia, came into existence. In Greek mythology, Gaia was among the deities who had the power to govern the entire universe, prior to the Titans' existence. In ancient times, she was known as the goddess who fulfilled everyone's dreams and was also responsible for the nourishment of young children and plants. Thus, Gaia was best known as the all nourishing and all producing mother. She was the only source of rising vapors that produced divine inspiration. In Homer's famous poem, 'The Iliad,' Gaia was revealed as a divine character. People took oaths to call upon her as well as sacrificed black sheep to her.

As per the creation story, grains and fruits are the symbols of the Mother Goddess. She is also known by the names of Chthon and Ge. For possessing an appearance similar to a mother, Gaia governed over oaths and marriages. Besides being worshipped as the Mother Goddess, she also gained the honor of a prophetess. Various renowned temples dedicated to the goddess Gaia are situated in Sparta, Athens, Olympia, Phylus, Tegea, Bura, and more.

Being the mother of creation, Gaia alone created the star-studded heavens in the form of the Father of the Sky, named Uranus. She not only created the Sky God but also the gigantic and towering mountains, along with the vast Sea. Hesiod stated that the Mother Earth created Uranus to be her equal. He was the universe's first king and wrapped himself around Gaia. Thus, Uranus became the husband of the goddess of Earth. Together, Gaia and Uranus became the ancestors of nearly all other Greek gods.

As a husband, Uranus was extremely cruel. As a father, he was even more brutal. He had an immense hatred towards his children, and for that reason, he never wanted his children to see the bright day's light. He fathered almost eighteen offspring with Gaia and would imprison each child by returning him or her to the womb of their mother. Uranus always rejoiced in such evil activities. On the other hand, Gaia loved her children and was grief-stricken by Uranus' actions.

The union of Uranus and Gaia gave birth to the Titans, who were twelve in number. The Titans were Oceanus, Coeus, Hyperion, Crius, Theia, Lapetus, Themis, Rhea, Phoebe, Mnemosyne, Tethys, and lastly, Cronus. Cronus, who was the youngest and last of the Titans, was extremely courageous and the most powerful.

Then, from Gaia and Uranus's union, the other gods who came forth were the Cyclopes who were born with excellent heart and immense force. The three Cyclopes were the 'thundering,' Brontes, the 'violent heart,' Arges and the 'flashing,' Steropes. The Cyclopes were similar to all other immortal gods with the only exception being that the three of them possessed only a single eye. The shape of the eye was round, and it was placed in the center of their foreheads.

The other children who took birth from the Sky God and Mother Earth were the Hecatoncheires, named Cottus, Gyges, and Briareos. All three of the Hecatoncheires were the creatures of ultimate arrogance. A total number of one hundred massive arms bulged out from their terrible shoulders, and 50 heads grew over the limbs. Thus, as a result of their intense strength and hideous appearance, the three of them were called by the name 'Hecatoncheires' which translates to 'hundred-handed ones'.

Gaia was disgusted by Uranus's evil actions. For that reason, Mother Earth plotted an evil and cunning plan of her own. She made a big scythe to attack her husband with. Then she explained everything to her children and requested their help. However, the only one with the courage to do so was her youngest son, Cronus. Both Cronus and Gaia set up a trap for the Father of the Sky. When Gaia met with Uranus that night, Cronus emerged out of his hiding place. With the scythe, Cronus castrated his father, casting his testicles into the sea. Uranus cursed his children, and for the first time he gave them the name 'Titans'.

From Uranus' blood, which was received by Gaia, various other creatures took birth. These creatures included Giants, Erinyes and Meliae. The Giants carried long spears and wore bronze armor. The Giants were powerful and had the ability to conduct war against all other gods. The 'Ash Tree Nymphs' known as the Meliae were sad creatures and offered their incorruptible hardwood for creating javelins and spears. The Erinyes, who were also known by the name the Furies, also took birth from Uranus's blood. The mighty Erinyes were Tisiphone (the vengeful), Alekto (the relentless), and Megaera (the jealous). They were winged witches whose hair changed into snakes. The Erinyes, who sought both justice and vengeance, were known to torture people that had committed murder, especially against their own families.

Uranus' severed genitals wandered for a prolonged time in the sea until they hit an island named Kythera. They mixed with the sea foam surrounding the island, and a beautiful girl possessing blonde hair arose from that foam. She was given the name of

'Aphrodite' by the gods. Aphrodite was the goddess of love and was highly respected by both immortals and men alike.

Taking over from the defeated Uranus, the next ruler was none other than Cronus. According to some versions of the creation myth, it is said that Cronus was able to liberate the other Titans. However, he was unable to free the Hecatoncheires and the Cyclopes from their imprisonment in Tartarus, a section of the Underworld that Uranus had banished them to.

The Lineage of Pontus

Pontus was considered to be the primitive God of the sea. He was also known to be the Father of fish as well as other creatures of the sea. Pontus was not just the deity of the sea; in fact, he himself was the sea, specifically the Mediterranean Sea. The meaning of the word Pontus is the 'road,' and the Greeks claimed the Mediterranean Sea to be their road for trading goods. He possesses a bearded face and two horns on his head that appear similar to the claws of a crab. According to Hesiod's version of events, Pontus was born from Gaia.

Pontus and his mother, Gaia, gave birth to five offspring. They were Thaumas, Eurybia, Phorcys, Nereus, and Ceto. Nereus was associated with the Aegean Sea and was often referred to as the Old Man of the Sea. He was well known for his virtuous and truthful nature. Nereus united with a sea nymph named Doris, and together they created fifty water nymphs, or Nereids.

Thaumas was Pontus's second son, who was the God of wonders as well as the dangers of the sea. He partnered with Electra, a cloud nymph. Together they produced the whirlwinds, named Harpies or Harpyiai, and also Iris. Iris was the Olympian gods' messenger and also the rainbow. Iris had a twin sister whose name was Arke. She was the Titan gods' messenger and the shadow of a rainbow.

Eurybia was Gaia and Pontus's daughter, who was known as a goddess who possessed a mastery over the seas. Basically, she had power over certain external factors such as winds, constellations, and weather. The Titan god named Krios was her partner, and together they gave birth to Pallas, Perses, and Astraeus.

Another offspring of Pontus was Phorcys, who was referred to as the god of big sea creatures and also dangers related to the sea. His counterpart was his sister named Ceto. Their offspring turned out to be the most threatening sea monsters. They were Echidna (sea dragon), Ladon (serpent with one-hundred heads), Graeae (seafoam hags with one eye), Thoosa (mother of Cyclops), and Scylla (big crab that attacked passing sailors). The Gorgons were also among the offspring of Ceto and Phorcys, one of them being the infamous Medusa. With their frightening, long, and fixed stare, they created dangerous reefs and rocks.

The Golden Age of the Titans

In Greek mythology, the golden age began soon after Uranus was killed by his son Cronus, who was one of the Titans. During this period, Cronus ruled over the cosmos along with his sister, Rhea. This age was full of prosperity and order, and everyone existed in harmony.

The individuals who took birth in this age were known to be the Golden Race, and they were created from Gaia. Sorrow and illness did not prevail during this age, and humans lived for nearly five hundred years. Nobody had to work in that period. Not only did the people live long lives, but they also did not physically age and deteriorate. There was no division between the rich and the poor, and every single person was a friend of the other.

During the golden age, or more specifically during the reign of Cronus, innocence and happiness were the norm. People had no need for houses as the days were warm and void of any scary things or dangerous. This particular age ended after the Titanomachy, otherwise known as the Titan War. This war was a long period of conflict between the Titans and younger gods.

In the Titanomachy, the Titans were overthrown by Zeus and were sent to Tartarus.

The Thread of Fate

Cronus's revolution against his father gave rise to the new cosmos. From that time onwards, both misfortune and violence became a part of the world. During the time of Cronus's reign, Nyx, who personified the night, created several sinister deities. The deities to whom Nyx gave birth were Thanatos (the death), Moros (the fate), Oneiroi (host of all dreams), Hypnos (the sleep), and Ker (black misfortune).

Nyx also created Oizys (unfortunate misery) and Momos (the blame). After that came forth Nemesis (the dreadful revenge), Philotes (the friendship), Apate (the deception), Eris (encounter with a brutal heart), Geras (the disastrous old age), and lastly Keres (heartless in offering penalties). They are the creatures that symbolize the most confusing, repulsive as well as bitter aspects of one's life. Men mostly avoid such aspects intentionally unless they are pressurized in doing so.

Birth of Zeus

Cronus learned of a prophecy that just like his father, he himself would be overthrown by one of his children. In a bid to avoid fulfilling the prophecy, he swallowed each of his children as they were born. Before Zeus's birth, Rhea and Cronus had already created five children, but they were all inside Cronus's stomach. When Rhea was about to give birth to Zeus, she requested that Gaia and Uranus help her. According to their instruction, she went away to Crete and hid inside a cave of the Cretan Mountains. Rhea gave birth to Zeus secretly. She sank her fingers inside the earth to suppress her cries. Ten Dactyls, who were the generous dwellers of the Cretan Mountains arose from Rhea's ten fingers. While she was giving birth, the Curetes were guarding the cave's entrance. Just after Zeus's birth, his mother handed him over to the Curetes. To cover the sound of the child's crying, they clashed shields, beat drums, stamped, and danced. To deceive Cronus, Rhea provided a cloth wrapped around a stone instead of the new-born baby. Cronus unknowingly swallowed the stone at once, thinking it was his new-born son.

Meanwhile, the God of lightning, thunder, and the sky was slowly growing up in the hidden cave of Crete. Melissa, the nymph, and Amalthea, the goat, played a crucial role in Zeus' upbringing. Zeus was nursed by Melissa, who took care of him. To help Zeus grow up more quickly, she fed him her wholesome honey. Previously, Amalthea had breastfed the sacred infant.

End of Cronus

Upon reaching adulthood, the Father of all gods of Mount Olympus, Zeus, came forward to rescue his own sisters and brothers. He united with the goddess of deep thought and wisdom, named Metis. She gave Zeus a combination of wine and mustard. Zeus secretly mixed the elixir into Cronus's drink. This caused Cronus to vomit out all five grown-up children. After liberating his siblings from the belly of his father, Zeus declared war against him. Along with his brothers and sisters, Poseidon, Hestia, Hera, Hades, and Demeter, Zeus fought against the Titans who allied with Cronus. Zeus also freed the Cyclopes as well as the Hecatonchires, who after being released fought on his side. The Titanomachy that lasted for ten long years, eventually ended with the victory of the Olympians and defeat of the Titans. The prophecy came true, and Cronus was sent to Tartarus along with the other Titans (except Prometheus) by his own son. Zeus sent Cronus there instead of killing him so that he would be forced to suffer eternal punishment.

Ages of Man

In accordance with Greek mythology, the entire humankind went through various eras. Each era was characterized by particular events. In ancient Greece, those eras were termed the 'ages of man.' Hesiod, the famous Greek poet, claimed that man passed through five such eras, and thus there were five ages of man. The five ages were the golden age, the silver age, the bronze age, the heroic age, or the age of heroes, and lastly, the iron age.

1. **Golden Age** - This was the first and, more importantly, the only age that fell under Cronus's rule. In this age, human beings lived very happily and peacefully among all the gods. Not only did they survive with the gods, but they also interacted and mingled with them. Nature provided plenty of food, and so there was no need for the people to work. Nobody ever became sad or unhappy. The season of Spring never seemed to end during this period. Thus, people of the golden age lived for many years, and they died harmoniously. The Golden Age came to an end after Zeus, alongside his siblings, defeated the Titans.

2. **Silver Age** - This age, and all the ages that follow, fell under Zeus's reign, the successor and son of Cronus. According to Hesiod, Zeus was the king of the whole universe and also the God or father of the other gods. He categorized a year into four separate seasons. In this age, people had to go to work. They had to plant grains as well as build proper shelters. Prior to growing up, a child

of this era could play and stay under his or her mother's dominion for as long as a hundred years. But, after becoming adults, they survived only for a short time because they clashed with one another regularly. They neither worshipped the gods, nor did they pay them any tribute, and for that reason, they all were killed by Zeus. People of the silver age became the underworld's 'blessed spirits' after dying.

3. **Bronze Age** - Individuals of this age were tough and hardened because their one passion and purpose was war. Such humans were created by Zeus from the ash tree. Their tools, homes, and armor were forged by bronze. The Deucalion's flood brought an end to this age.

4. **Heroic Age** - The heroes of the Heroic Age fought at Troy and Thebes. The humans of this era went away to Elysium after their death.

5. **Iron Age** - In this age, people led a life of misery and toil. Children disrespected their parents, the social connection between guests and hosts almost diminished, and brother fought with brother.

The Universal Flood

In accordance with Greek mythology, every single God helped in submerging the entire world. To be very specific, the most assistance was provided by Poseidon. It rained continuously for a prolonged period. For that reason, almost all the people on earth died. After that, the nereids came out of the sea. After their emergence, they saw the woods as well as the nymphs, who were their earthly sisters. They all rushed hastily and hid in the depth of water as men called out for their help. The reason behind their withdrawal was that they were not permitted to assist the men.

The only dry place on earth was the elevated peak of Mount Parnassus. It rose just like a minute island. All around the summit was nothing other than the infinite and endless sea. After a time, a boat was seen advancing towards the emerged peak of Parnassus. On the boat, a total number of two living individuals were present. Jupiter spared both of them because of their goodness. One of them was Prometheus's only son named Deucalion, and the other one was Pyrrha, Epimetheus, and the enchantress Pandora's daughter.

Both of them had survived and sailed in the boat for a continuous stretch of nine days. As they landed on Mount Parnassus, they soon realized that they were the only two people still alive. Water was pulled back gradually, and the earth slowly arose, glittered in bright sunlight. The rivers returned, and the intense silence broke. Deucalion and Pyrrha had doubts about what to do in such emptiness and loneliness. They noticed the temple of an ancient Titaness, Themis. The temple was near the river Cephissus's mouth. Themis was often personified as fairness, divine order, custom, and natural law. Both Deucalion and Pyrrha visited her temple to request her assistance in reforming the entire human race. The goddess Themis ordered them to leave her temple and throw the great mother's bones behind them with loosened clothes and veiled heads. At first, both of them felt extremely confused, but later they understood that 'great mother' was referring to none other than Mother Earth, Gaia. By bones, the goddess Themis meant stones.

They both acted according to Themis's instructions. All the stones that Pyrrha threw behind her became women, and the ones thrown by Deucalion became men. Those women and men repopulated the entire world. Other animals were gradually produced from the earth.

Over time, Deucalion settled along with Pyrrha in Thessaly. There the couple had two children. The names of their offspring were Amphictyon and Hellen. Hellen went on to give birth to the originator of the Dorians, named Dorus, Aeolus the creator of the Aeolians, and Xuthus. Later, Xuthus gave birth to the founder of the Ionians, whose name was Ion, and also to Achaeus the originator of the Achaeans.

Chapter 2: Greek Gods and Goddesses

The ancient Greeks worshipped multiple gods and goddesses – that is, they were polytheistic. A majority of their gods and goddesses resided at the top of Mount Olympus, which is the highest mountain in Greece. According to the myths, the gods often actively got involved in the day-to-day activities of humans. These myths helped explain the unknown as well as teach the people of ancient Greece lessons about life and morality.

Several stories regarding how the Greek gods interacted and behaved around humans can be found in the works of Homer. He wrote two epic poems – the Odyssey, which described the travels of the hero Odysseus, and the Iliad, which described the events of the Trojan War. These two epic poems were orally passed down over several generations.

In this chapter, we will discuss Greek mythology's most prominent gods and their impact on the people of ancient Greece.

Zeus – The King of the Gods and the God of the Sky

Zeus was an extremely imposing figure and was considered the first of the Gods. He was often referred to as the "Father of Gods and men" and was a sky god who could control thunder and lightning. He offered omens and signs, managed the weather, and dispensed justice to guarantee order amongst both the mortals and the gods. He did all of this from his seat, which was situated high on Mount Olympus.

Zeus's mother was Rhea, and his father was Cronus. Cronus had swallowed all his previous children (Poseidon, Hades, Hera, Demeter, and Hestia) to prevent any takeover as he had been told that one of his children would usurp him. As we talked about earlier, Zeus was hidden from Cronus and eventually went on to rescue his siblings, as well as overthrow his father.

Zeus, along with Poseidon and Hades, became the king of Olympus and shared the rule of the world. They even followed him into The Battle of the Titans. Zeus mated with several mortals and goddesses, but was married to his sister Hera who was the goddess of marriage.

Zeus was revered by all as the king of gods who sat on the golden throne on Mount Olympus. Mortal kings would often boast that they were Zeus' descendants. Along with this supreme power, he also held various roles and responsibilities. According to Hesiod, Zeus was the "lord of justice" who brought peace instead of violence. He was the supreme cultural embodiment of Greek religious beliefs and was popularly known as the god of sky and thunder. He had several titles or epithets that emphasized the various aspects of his wide range of authorities.

According to Hesiod's "Work and Days," Zeus was a carefree God who loved laughing out loud. He was prudent, merciful, just, fair, wise, and unpredictable. He is generally described as a strong and imposing god who had long, curly hair and a regal body. He usually is depicted with a scruff or a short beard and is always carrying his thunderbolt with him.

Hera – The Queen of Olympus and the Goddess of Marriage

Hera was the wife of Zeus and the queen of Olympus and the Greek gods. She was the goddess of marriage and family, and represented an ideal woman. However, she was more famous for her vengeful and jealous behavior, which was mostly aimed against her husband's lovers and his illegitimate offspring. She symbolized monogamy and fidelity as she was one of the very few goddesses who remained faithful to her partner.

According to Greek mythology, Hera was Cronus' and Rhea's daughter, and also the mother of Eileithyia (goddess of childbirth), Hebe (goddess of youth), and Ares (god of war). In retaliation for Zeus' single-handed birth of Athena, she also gave birth to Hephaistos (god of metallurgy) alone. However, because of Hephaistos' ugliness, she threw him from Mount Olympus and sent him crashing to Earth.

Hera had to battle with the infidelities of her husband regularly, and she took swift revenge. She was also known to turn her anger towards humans. For instance, she cursed Paris, who choose Aphrodite over Hera as the most beautiful deity at Thetis's marriage to the mortal Peleus.

Hera is portrayed in statues and images as being solemn and majestic, and crowned with the polos, which is a tall cylindrical crown worn by several Great Goddesses. She ruled over the heavens as well as the Earth even before she was married to Zeus. This is why she is often referred to as the "Queen of Heaven".

Everyone feared Hera, including the great Zeus. She had no concept of justice when she got jealous or angry. She never forgave the women with whom Zeus engaged in sexual relations, even when they were innocent of any wrongdoing. Her never-ending hatred for Zeus' illegitimate son Hercules was legendary. Hera even tried to kill Hercules by raising a storm while he was at sea. Zeus became so enraged that as punishment he hung her in the clouds with a golden chain and tied heavy anvils to her legs.

Hades – The King of the Underworld and the God of the Dead

Hades was not only the name of the ancient Greek god of the underworld, but it was also used to describe a shadowy place beneath the Earth, which was considered to be the home of the dead. Both Hesiod and Homer describe Hades as the most feared of the gods, and as 'monstrous,' 'loathsome,' and 'pitiless.' He was the oldest son of Cronus and Rhea. He abducted Persephone to join him in the underworld and got married to her. His symbol is a cornucopia, or scepter.

After the Olympian gods overthrew the Titans and the Giants, Hades drew lots with his brothers Poseidon and Zeus in order to decide the parts of the world each god would rule. While Poseidon received the seas, and Zeus received the sky, Hades got the underworld. Even though Hades was a less prominent protagonist in the stories of Greek mythology as compared to the other Olympian gods, he was held in superstitious awe by the Greek people. Speaking his name was avoided; instead, epithets like Eubuleus (giving good advice) were used. There were also stories about sacrificial practices that were carried out at night in honor of Hades. The blood of the victims was allowed to seep down into the earth to reach the underworld god.

Hades was the sole god who did not reside on Mount Olympus and instead lived in the Underworld. He had a helmet made by Hephaistos, which could make the wearer invisible. This helmet was used by Athena in the Trojan War when she fought Ares, as well as by Perseus in his quest for Medusa's head.

In Classical and Archaic art, Hades is mostly represented as a bearded, mature man, holding a scepter, a libation vase, a 2-pronged spear, or a cornucopia, which is the symbol of vegetable and mineral wealth which comes from the ground. He is also often depicted riding on a chariot pulled by black-colored horses along with Persephone, or as seated on an ebony throne.

It was believed that the god Hermes led souls to the Styx River in the Underworld. From this point, Charon, an aged boatman, ferried them to the gates of Hades. The gates were guarded by a ferocious 3-headed dog called Kerberos whose job was to keep the souls inside. The Underworld was not really a place of suffering and torture; instead, it was just the souls' final resting place. Even though it was a fearful place to the mortals, several heroes would often visit Hades in the underworld during their adventures.

Poseidon – The God of the Sea

In ancient Greek religion, Poseidon was the god of the sea, horses, storms, and earthquakes. He is considered one of the most greedy, moody, and bad-tempered among the Olympian gods. He was also known to turn vengeful when he was insulted. The name Poseidon either suggests "lord of the earth" or "husband of the earth." He is differentiated from Pontus, the oldest Greek deity of the waters and the personification of the sea.

Poseidon was the son of Cronus and Rhea. He was swallowed by his father Cronus along with Hera, Hestia, Demeter, and Hades. In some folklore stories, however, it is said that like Zeus, Poseidon was not swallowed by Cronus as his mother Rhea had saved him as well. It is believed that Rhea had pretended to have given birth to a colt and hidden Poseidon among a flock of lambs. Cronus had devoured the colt instead of Poseidon.

After defeating their father, Poseidon was given the kingdom of the sea to rule over. His main symbol and weapon was the trident, which might have once been a fishing spear. The poet, Hesiod, said that the trident of Poseidon was designed by the three Cyclopes, similar to Hades' helmet and Zeus' thunderbolt.

Poseidon was regarded as the god of earthquakes as well as the god of dry lands. In Greece, he was mostly worshipped in inland regions, although these regions were centered around streams and pools, or connected with bodies of water in some way. Inland, he used to be worshipped as *asphalios* ("stabilizer") and *ennosigiaos* ("earth-shaker"). Being the god of horses, he is thought to have been introduced to Greece by the earliest Hellenes. They were also thought to have introduced the first horses into Greece in the second century BCE. Poseidon also fathered several horses, among which the winged horse Pegasus was the best known.

Poseidon came into conflict over several land disputes with a variety of figures. One of the most notable among them was the contest for jurisdiction over Attica. Poseidon lost it to the goddess Athena. Although he lost Attica, he was still worshipped there, at Colonus in particular, where he was known as *hippios* ("of horses").

Isthmia was the chief festival celebrated in honor of Poseidon. This festival of famous athletic contests (such as horse races) was celebrated near the Isthmus of Corinth in alternating years. His role as a sea god gradually became prominent in art, and the attributes of the tuna, the dolphin, and the trident were used to represent him.

Ares – The God of War

In Greek religion, Ares represented the god of war. As opposed to Mars (his Roman counterpart), he was not very popular and was not extensively worshipped in Greece. Instead, he was simply considered to be the spirit of battle. He was one of the 12 Olympian Gods, and Homer described him as Zeus and Hera's son.

In literature, Ares represented the brutal and disrespectful aspects of warfare and slaughter, which was opposite to the goddess Athena who represented generalship and military strategy as the goddess of intelligence. Even though Ares symbolized the physical aggression that is essential for success in warfare, the Greeks were not fond of him because he was a threatening and devastating force that was insatiable in battle. Even his parents were not fond of him. Nonetheless, his sons Deimos, Phobos, and his sister Eris accompanied him in battles. Two lesser war deities Enyo and Enyalius, were also associated with him. Enyalius is virtually identical to Ares himself, while Enyo is his female equivalent.

In Greece, Ares was mostly worshipped in the northern regions. His cult had several unique local characteristics, even though it was devoid of theological, moral, and social associations. In early times, human sacrifices were made in his honor from among the prisoners of war in Sparta. In addition to this, an unusual nocturnal offering of dogs was made to him as Enyalius, which might indicate an infernal or chthonic deity. At Athens, there was a temple in his honor at the foot of the Areopagus hills, which were also known as "Ares' Hills."

He was well known in the literature as Aphrodite's lover. Aphrodite was married to Hephaestus, but was also Ares' legitimate wife at one point, and he fathered Harmonia, Phobos, Deimos, and Eros with her. He fathered Alcippe with Aglauros, who was the daughter of Cecrops.

Hermes – The God of Trade and Eloquence

Hermes was the ancient god of trade, travel, thieves, language, sleep, animal husbandry, fertility, luck, wealth, border crossings, and was a guide to the underworld. Considered as one of the most mischievous and cunning of the 12 Olympian gods, Hermes was the herald and messenger of Mount Olympus, inventor of the lyre, and the patron of the shepherds. He was the 2nd youngest Olympian god and was the son of Zeus and Maia. Maia was the daughter of the Titan Atlas, and one of the 7 Pleiades.

Hermes was often identified with the Roman Mercury, and with Cadmilus or Casmilus, one of the Cabeiri. His name is believed to be derived from the Greek word herma, which means 'heap of stones'. The word was used in the country to specify landmarks or boundaries. Some of the first centers of his cult were located in Arcadia. Mount Cyllene was thought to be his birthplace, and at Mount Cyllene, his images were ithyphallic, and there he was worshipped as the god of fertility.

He was associated with the protection of sheep and cattle in his cult, as well as in literature, and was often linked with the deities of vegetation, particularly the nymphs, and Pan. However, in the Odyssey, he mainly appears as the conductor of the dead to Hades, and the messenger to the gods. Hermes was also considered as a dream god, and the Greeks used to make an offering to him before going to sleep. To some, he was also known as the god of doorways and roads, as well as the protector of travelers. Any stroke of good luck was credited to him, and any treasure casually found was thought to be his gift. He was considered to be Apollo's counterpart in several respects: similar to him, Hermes was also an advocate of music and was attributed to the creation of the kithara and, at times, of music itself. Hermes was also a god of eloquence and took charge of some kinds of popular divination.

In ancient art, Hermes is depicted as a mature man with a beard. He is typically shown with winged boots, a cap on his head, and wearing a long tunic. He was sometimes also portrayed in his pastoral character with a sheep on his shoulder. At the end of the fifth century BCE, however, he was portrayed as a young, naked, athlete who did not have a beard.

Apollo – The God of the Sun, Light, Prophecy, and Music

Apollo is a God who has several meanings and functions in Greco-Roman mythology and is one of the most influential and respected of all the ancient Greek and Roman deities. Although his real nature is unknown, he was seen as the god of divine distance who did things from afar. He was considered one of the most complex gods and was seen as the god of knowledge, light, Sun, plague, medicine, oracles, art archery, and music. He was the god who presided over the constitutions and religious laws of the country, and also was the one who made humans aware of their own guilt and wrongdoings. He was also known to communicate with mortals through oracles and prophets.

Born to his father Zeus and mother Leto (a Titan) on the Greek island of Delos, Apollo was feared by all gods. Only Zeus and Leto could endure his presence with ease. He was also a god of herds and crops, mainly as a divine defense for diseases and wild animals, as is indicated by his Greek epithet Alexikakos or the Averter of Evil. He was also linked with the Sun as his first name was Phoebus, which indicates "pure" or "bright." Nomios (Herdsman) was another of his Greek epithets. It is believed that as a punishment for killing Zeus' armorers, the Cyclopes, he served King Admetus of Pharae in the lowly position of groom and herdsman.

In art, Apollo was portrayed as a beardless youth, either wearing a robe or naked. His symbolic bow represented a summation of awe, terror, death, and distance. However, another gentler side of his nature was depicted through his other attribute, the lyre, which showed his joy of communion with Olympus through dance, poetry, and music. Hermes had created the lyre for him, and it became one of his most notable attributes. Both Zeus and Leto were proud of their son, who radiated with grace.

Athena – The Goddess of War and Wisdom

In Greek mythology, Athena (also known as Athene) was the protector of the city and the goddess of practical reason, handicraft, war, wisdom, inspiration, arts, crafts, skill, strategy, mathematics, strategic warfare, law and justice, civilization, inspiration, and courage. More specifically, she is known for her strategic skills in warfare and is often depicted as a companion of several heroes. Because of her adventures she is considered the patron goddess of heroic ventures.

Athena was Zeus' daughter, who was thought to be born after Zeus experienced an extreme headache. She is believed to have sprung fully grown from his forehead, clothed in armor. She is motherless, although one of the most popularly cited pieces of folklore suggests that Zeus laid with Metis, the goddess of wisdom and prudence. Shortly after, Zeus heard of a prophecy proclaiming that she would have a son that would go on to overthrow Zeus. To avoid the prophecy from playing out, Zeus tricked her into transforming into a fly, and then swallowed her whole! A few months later, Athena sprung from Zeus' forehead, leading some to believe that Metis was her mother.

Athena had immense power and she quickly became Zeus' favorite child. She was portrayed carrying a lance and a shield and wearing body armor. In Homer's Iliad, she is described as a war goddess who inspired and fought alongside several Greek heroes. Her help is synonymous with her military prowess. She represents the civilized and intellectual side of war as well as the virtues of skill and justice, whereas Ares depicts purely blood lust. This is where her military and moral superiority comes from when compared to Ares. She is portrayed as the divine form of martial and heroic ideals, and personifies greatness in close combat, triumph, and glory. Athena became the goddess of practical insight, of prudent restraint, and of good counsel.

Aphrodite – The Goddess of Love and Eternal Beauty

In ancient Greek literature, Aphrodite is the goddess of beauty and love. *Aphros, in Greek,* means "foam," and in *Theogony,* Hesiod suggests that Aphrodite was born from the white foam that was produced in the waters of Paphos, which is situated around the island of Cyprus. The white foam was believed to have been produced from the severed genitals of Uranus when the Titan Cronus had thrown them into the sea. However, as indicated in Homer's *Iliad*, Aphrodite might also have been Zeus and Dione's daughter.

In early Greek art, Aphrodite is portrayed to be fully clothed and without any special features that could separate her from other goddesses. She was widely worshipped as the goddess of the sea as well as of seafaring. People also respected and honored her as the goddess of war in several places, particularly Cyprus, Thebes, and Sparta. However, she was mainly known as a goddess of sexual love and fertility. She also presided over marriages, occasionally.

Many deities thought that she was so beautiful that a rivalry over her could start a war among the gods. Zeus married her to Hephaestus for this reason, as he was ugly and deformed. In spite of her marriage to Hephaestus, Aphrodite had several lovers, which included both gods and humans. The most important of Aphrodite's mortal lovers was the Trojan shepherd Anchises. She became the mother of Adonis and Aeneas. Among the gods, she had an affair with Ares, the god of war.

Artemis – The Goddess of the Moon, Forest, and Hills

In Greek religion, Artemis was believed to be the goddess of childbirth, chastity, vegetation, the hunt, and wild animals. She was also referred to as the goddess of the moon, at times. The favorite goddess among the rural population, she was the daughter of Leto and Zeus, and was Apollo's twin sister. Her functions and character greatly varied from one region to another. However, across all regions she was known as the goddess of wild nature, who danced in marshes, forests, and mountains accompanied by the nymphs. She also protected young children and was known to alleviate diseases in women.

Artemis was a virgin, and this drew the interest and attention of several men and gods. However, only Orion, who was her hunting companion, was able to win her heart. It was thought that Orion was killed accidentally by Gaia, or by Artemis herself. The poets after Homer stressed upon her chastity and her interest in shadowy groves, music, dancing, and hunting.

The wrath of Artemis was well known. She was known to act out in anger whenever someone disobeyed her wishes, especially if someone harmed the animals that were sacred to her. In one version of Adonis' stories, it was told that Artemis had tried to kill Adonis by sending a wild boar after him because he claimed that he was a better hunter than she was.

Greek sculptures, however, avoided depicting her unpitying anger as a motif.

In ancient Greek art, Artemis is most commonly portrayed as a beautiful maiden huntress carrying a bow and a quiver or, alternatively, a spear. On occasion, she dons a feline skin and is seen accompanied by a hunting dog, stag, or a deer. Earlier representations also symbolize her role as the goddess of animals and show her with wings and with an animal or bird in each hand.

Chapter 3: Demi-Gods

In Greek mythology, the term demi-god is used to describe someone who has one human parent and one divine parent. The divine parent might be a major Olympian god or a lesser one, like a nymph. It was believed that demi-gods had special abilities that were far beyond those of a normal mortal. As a result, several demi-gods of Greek mythology were worshipped as heroes.

Achilles

In Greek mythology, Achilles was the leader of the fearsome Myrmidons, slayer of Hector, and sacker of cities. He was the most handsome and bravest warrior in the army of Agamemnon in the Trojan War. He was quite simply invincible on the battlefield. However, he was too proud and ill-tempered, and his reckless anger would often cost both his enemies as well as his countrymen their lives.

Achilles was believed to be born to Thetis, the Nereid, and Peleus, who was the King of the Myrmidons. It was said that both Zeus and Poseidon fell in love with Thetis, however, when Prometheus reminded them of the prophecy that stated that Thetis' son would become greater than his father, the Olympian gods decided to not pursue a relationship with her. This led to

Thetis marrying Peleus. When Achilles was born, his mother dipped him in the Styx River in order to make him immortal. She dipped him in, holding him by the heels, and since his heels didn't touch the water, it remained the only region of his body that could be harmed.

An Oracle told King Peleus that his son Achilles would die fighting at Troy. Thetis tried to hide Achilles away from the world because she knew that he was fated to have a short but glorious life. Thus, the boy was brought up in Skyros with the royal family of Lycomedes. He was safe there for a time, up until the soothsayer Calchas told the Greek gods that they could not take Troy without Achilles. Trusting the advice of Calchas, the gods searched for Achilles and recruited him in their war efforts.

During the first nine years of the Trojan War, Achilles took twelve cities and ravaged the country around Troy. In the tenth year, there was an argument between Achilles and Agamemnon which led to Achilles refusing to provide his services. Without him on the battlefield the Greeks struggled badly. Achilles let Patroclus impersonate him by lending him his armor and chariot. However, Patroclus was killed by the eldest son of King Priam of Troy.

Having finally reunited with Agamemnon, Hephaestus (the god of metallurgy) gave Achilles new armor, and after that, he killed

Hector. He then dragged Hector's dead body behind his chariot. On King Priam's earnest plea, Achilles returned Hector's body to him.

It was believed that Achilles was killed in battle shortly after by Paris (Priam's son). It was said that Paris' arrow was guided by the god Apollo, striking him in his heel, the one place where he was vulnerable to attack.

Arcas

Arcas was the son of Callisto and the legendary king of Greek mythology, Zeus. Callisto was the daughter of the King Lycaon of Pelasgia. Callisto was seduced by Zeus, not in her father's palace, but in the woods as she was a part of Artemis' hunting group. When Artemis, the virgin goddess, realized that one of her attendants had gotten pregnant, she expelled Callisto from her hunting group. There was worse to come for Callisto though. Hera became jealous and angry when she gave birth to Zeus' son, and transformed her into a bear. Thus, Callisto was left to wander like a wild animal in the woods in which she once used to hunt. The same fate would have befallen Zeus and Callisto's son, or she might even have killed him if Zeus had not stepped in and whisked the newborn baby away.

The newborn baby was named Arcas, and Zeus gave him to the messenger god Hermes. Arcas was subsequently raised to adulthood by Hermes' mother, the Pleiad Maia.

Zeus got into a disagreement with king Lycaon, Arcas' maternal grandfather. In his anger, Zeus transformed the King into a werewolf. Arcas then became the new King of Pelasgia, which would later be renamed Arcadia, in his honor.

Arcas was believed to be a good king. He introduced his masses to basket weaving, bread making, and crop cultivation. Triptolemus, the disciple of Demeter, had taught Arcus the agricultural arts. Arcas fathered at least three sons, Elatus, Azan, and Apheidas. However, several other children of Arcas are named as well, including Triphylus, Peiasgus, Hyperippe, Erymanthus, Deiomeneia, and Autolaus.

Apart from being interested in agriculture, he was also good at hunting – a skill that he inherited from his mother. The king of Arcadia would often go hunting in the same jungles that his mother, Callisto, once hunted in. One day, while hunting, Arcas met his transformed mother. Although Callisto immediately recognized her son and came forward to hug him, Arcas could not identify his mother and prepared to kill the bear approaching him with his bow and arrow. Zeus, who was watching the events from Mount Olympus, wished to stop the tragedy of a son killing his mother and immediately converted Arcas into a bear. He further transformed them into two new constellations, Ursa Major and Ursa Minor.

Minos

In Greek Mythology, King Minos is considered to be one of the most famous kings after whom a whole civilization was named, which was known as the Minoan civilization. Arthur Evans, an archaeologist, came up with the name while working on the island of Crete, as King Minos was believed to have ruled there.

The tale of King Minos is believed to have started with the popular tale of Europa's kidnapping by Zeus. Europa was a Phoenician princess. According to the story, Zeus transformed into a bull and abducted her from the shores of Phoenicia, taking her to the kingdom of Crete. Zeus then had his way with the beautiful Europa on the island of Crete beneath a Cypress tree, and as a result of their short affair, Europa gave birth to three sons – Minos, Rhadamanthys, and Sarpedon. Europa was then abandoned on Crete by Zeus. However, she prospered when she married Asterion, who was the king of Crete at that time. Europa's children were also adopted by Asterion, who raised them as his own.

When Asterion died, the question arose as to who among his sons would be the next king of Crete. Minos prayed to Poseidon, asking him to give him a sign. As a sign, a magnificent white bull accompanied by the gods emerged from the sea. After this, there was no doubt that Minos would be crowned the king of Crete. Minos further banished his brothers from Crete to make sure that no future questions regarding his legitimacy arose. Rhadamanthys later became the king of Boeotia, while Sarpedon became the king of Lycia.

It was said that King Minos' rule over Crete was lengthy and thriving, and it was believed that Zeus himself was guiding King Minos' sovereignty. During his rule, the importance of the kingdom of Crete greatly increased. He molded the navy of the kingdom and made it one of the most robust naval forces of the ancient world. A just and fair legal system by which all the citizens were treated equally was also believed to have been introduced during the sovereignty of King Minos. The Cretan laws were so well designed that it was said that other city-states like Corinth and Sparta often consulted Minos regarding the re-codification of their own laws.

Minos also acquired power over the Aegean islands with the help of Knossos and colonized many of them, while also eliminating the pirates in the sea. He got married to Helios' daughter, Pasiphae, who bore him Phaedra, Ariadne, and Androgeos, among others, and who was the mother of the Minotaur as well.

Helen

In Greek mythology, Helen of Troy was considered the most beautiful woman in Greece. She was known as the woman whose beauty triggered the Trojan War. However, Helen's character was far more complicated than that. A layered and fascinating woman emerges when you consider the several Greek and Roman myths that surround her – from when she was just a child to her life after the Trojan War.

Helen was also fathered by Zeus, who appeared in the form of a swan and either assaulted or seduced her mother, Leda. Leda slept with her husband Tyndareus on the same night and consequently gave birth to 4 children, which hatched from 2 eggs. The demi-gods Helen and Polydeuces came from one egg, while two mortals Castor and Clytemnestra came from the other egg. In another older myth, Helen was said to be the daughter of Zeus and Nemesis, who was the goddess of vengeance.

Helen was fated to become the most beautiful woman in the world. As a young child, she was kidnapped by the hero Theseus who wanted her to be his bride and hid her in the city of Athens. However, Helen's brothers rescued her and brought her home. Helen was courted by several suitors, from who she chose the King of Sparta, Menelaus. However, even though Menelaus was wealthy and valiant, Helen's love for him would prove to be weak.

The wedding of the goddess Thetis and the mortal Peleus was a great event among the Olympians. All the gods, except for Eris, were invited to the wedding. Furious at her exclusion, Eris attended anyway and tossed an apple towards Aphrodite, Athena, and Hera, saying the apple was "for the most beautiful". Each goddess claimed that the apple was meant for her. To settle their dispute over who was the most beautiful, Zeus told the Trojan prince Paris to decide who the most beautiful of the three was. Each goddess offered him a bribe to sway his vote. Paris chose Aphrodite as the winner because she had promised him that in return, she would make Helen become his wife.

Paris then traveled to the court of Menelaus to claim his prize. He was honored as a guest there. However, Paris seduced Helen and fled with her defying the old laws of hospitality. Paris sailed back to Troy with his new bride, and this act was considered to be abduction in spite of Helen's complicity. Menelaus, realizing that Helen was gone, led troops overseas to start a war against Troy along with his brother Agamemnon. After Paris was killed, Helen married his brother Deiphobus. However, once Troy was captured, Helen abandoned her new husband and returned to Sparta with Menelaus.

Chiron

In Greek mythology, Chiron was considered one of the wisest and the most important Centaurs. He was famous for his wisdom and teaching abilities. He was the son of the nymph

Philyra and the Titan god Cronus. Even though centaurs had the lower body of a horse and an upper body of a human, the front legs of Chiron were also human, which revealed that not only was he different than the rest of the centaurs, he was also higher in class than them. The other differences between Chiron and the other centaurs were that he was not overcome with lust, did not indulge in drinking, was far more civilized in nature, and had superior knowledge.

Chiron lived on Mount Pelion in Thessaly with his wife Chariclo, who was a nymph. They had a son who was named Carystus, as well as three daughters named Ocyrhoe, Endeis, and Hippe. Many famous Greek heroes and gods of Greek mythology were taught by him. His students included Perseus, Peleus, Jason, Theseus, Achilles, Ajax, Asclepius, and even Phoenix and Heracles.

His death was caused as a result of the events that began when Heracles, while trying to finish the 4th task given in the Labors of Heracles, visited the centaur Pholus in his cave. The two of them had supper, and when Heracles asked to drink some wine, Pholus opened a bottle of sacred wine that Dionysus had given to him. However, the wine's smell attracted the other centaurs that were present close by, and they attacked in an effort to get the wine for themselves. Heracles shot poisoned arrows and killed many of them. One of those arrows struck Chiron by mistake. Although Chiron was immortal and couldn't die, he was in unbearable pain because of the poison. Thus, when Heracles asked him to give up his immortality in order to free Prometheus, he happily did so, and then, he joined the gods on Mount Olympus.

Pelias

In Greek mythology, Pelias was the son of Tyro and the god Poseidon, and also was the king of the Iolcus. Some versions of the story say that he was married to Phylomache, while others claim that he was actually married to Anaxibia. Regardless of who he was in fact married to, he had a number of children with her, including Antinoe, Hippotheo, Pelopia, Alcestis, Pisidice, and Acastus.

Poseidon was in love with Tyro. However, Tyro liked Enipeus, who was a river god. So, Poseidon impersonated Enipeus and tricked Tyro to sleep with him. She got pregnant and gave birth to Neleus and Pelias. However, Tyro left them to die in the mountains where a herdsman found them and raised them. When Neleus and Pelias became adults, they looked for their mother and then killed her stepmother. Pelias wanted to be the sole ruler of Thessaly, and so he exiled Neleus, his brother, as well as his half-brother Pheres. He also imprisoned Aeson, his other half-brother. While he was imprisoned, Aeson got married and had several children, among whom was the famous

Jason. Aeson feared that Pelias might kill Jason, so he managed to disguise him and sent him away.

After receiving a prophecy from an oracle to be careful of a man wearing a single sandal, Pelias was very scared that someone might overthrow him. Then years later, Pelias arranged the Olympics in Iolcus in which Jason decided to participate. He lost one of his sandals on the way, and when he reached Iolcus, Pelias became aware of the presence of a stranger wearing a single sandal. Pelias was overcome with fear, and resultingly, hatched a plan to get rid of Jason. He gave Jason a seemingly deadly and impossible task of recovering the Golden Fleece from Colchis, in a garden which was guarded by a never-sleeping dragon. Pelias had agreed to give up his throne if Jason could return with the Golden Fleece.

Jason, guided by goddess Hera, gathered a band of heroes, which were known as the Argonauts, and set sail on a vessel, the Argo. After several adventures, Jason and the Argonauts managed to successfully retrieve the Golden Fleece and bring it back to Pelias. Pelias, however, refused to give up his throne to Jason when they returned. So, Medea, Jason's wife, made a plan to take revenge. She showed Pelias' daughters how they could give anyone their youth back simply by cutting them up and boiling them with some herbs. The daughters believed her and cut up Pelias and threw him in a pot of boiling water, thereby killing him.

Theseus

Theseus, a legendary hero of Greek mythology, was the son of either Poseidon (the sea god) or Aegeus (the king of Athens) and Aethra, the daughter of Pittheus. According to myth, as Aegeus was childless, Pittheus allowed him to have a child (Theseus) with his daughter Aethra. When Theseus was an adult, he found out his father's identity, upon which Aethra sent him to Athens.

He encountered several adventures on his journey to Athens. The first villain he came across was Periphetes, who killed anyone who came his way by smashing their heads with a huge iron club. Theseus killed him without any ceremony. Next came Sinis at the Isthmus of Corinth, who was called the Pine Bender as he used to kill people by tearing them apart with pine trees. Theseus killed Sinis with a bent pine tree itself. Theseus then dispatched Phaea, the Crommyonian Sow. He then flung the wicked Sciron off a cliff as Sciron himself used to kick his visitors into the sea after forcing them to wash his feet. After that, he came across Procrustes, who used to ambush travelers and attach them to a bed made of iron, and then kill them. Theseus killed him by putting him on his own device. In Megara, Theseus met the champion wrestler Cercyon, who used to force strangers to wrestle with him. Theseus killed him in a wrestling match.

After arriving in Athens, Theseus discovered that his father Aegeus was married to the sorceress Medea. Medea identified Theseus even before Aegeus did, and tried to convince her husband to poison Theseus. However, when Aegeus finally realized it was his son, he declared Theseus the heir to the throne of Athens. Medea and the Pallantidae (Theseus' cousins) tried to get rid of him several times but always fell short. Then, Medea sent him off to fight the fire-breathing bull of Marathon, who was terrorizing the countryside. Theseus captured the bull and gave it to Apollo.

Next came Theseus' most famous adventure of killing the Cretan Minotaur, half bull and half man. He had promised Aegeus that he would replace the black sail on his ship with a white-colored one if he successful. However, he forgot this promise he had made to his father and, Aegeus on seeing the black sail jumped off of a cliff, taking his own life.

Asclepius

Asclepius, the son of Apollo (the god of prophecy, truth, and healing) and the mortal princess Coronis, was considered to be the god of medicine, and the powers of divination were also assigned to him. According to a few stories, Apollo killed Coronis for being unfaithful, while in other versions, Coronis abandoned her baby near Epidaurus as she was ashamed of his illegitimacy. Apollo was then said to take care of the motherless Asclepius, giving him the gift of healing as well as the secrets of medicine with herbs and plants. He was also taught by the Centaur Chiron.

Asclepius had several children, including two sons: Podaleirios and Machaon, and four daughters: Aglaia, Aceso, Panacea, and Iaso. In some versions, he was married to Hygeia, another goddess of health, while in other versions, he was married to Epione, and Hygeia was his daughter.

Asclepius met a tragic end when he was struck by a thunderbolt thrown by Zeus, who was afraid that Asclepius could make all men immortal. He saw his medical prowess as a threat to the eternal separation between humans and gods, especially after hearing rumors that his healing powers were so good that he could even awaken the dead. Apollo protested against his son's murder. However, Zeus punished him as well for impiety and ordered him to serve Admetos, the king of Thessaly, for a year. Following his death, Asclepius was deified, and according to some local stories, he even became the constellation, Ophiuchus.

In ancient Greek art, Asclepius was portrayed on coins, in mosaics, pottery, and sculpture. He was almost always depicted as fully bearded, wearing a simple himation robe and with a staff in his hand that had a sacred snake coiled around it. In some forms, he is accompanied by Hygeia, and sometimes there's a dog at his feet. Asclepius was also associated with three different types of trees: olive, pine, and cypress.

Chapter 4: Heroes in Greek Mythology

According to Hesiod and Homer, mankind was divided into five ages. Zeus, the king of Olympus and the Greek gods, created a race of men in the fourth of these ages. These men that they created were mortals but were really powerful and noble. This Heroic age, which extended for almost six generations as per ancient genealogy, was the period for the legendary figures like Aeneus, Orpheus, Prometheus, Odysseus, Hector, Jason, and Heracles. All of the greatest heroes lived during this fourth age, which was a time of not only great adventures but bloodshed and turmoil as well.

Heroes in Greek mythology were all exceptional in one way or the other. They were God-like with special strength, courage, or ability. They were noted for their superhuman courageous acts and were often of divine ancestry. Some of the bravest heroes of Ancient Greece are as follows:

Hercules (Heracles)

Hercules (the Roman name for the Greek hero Heracles) is one of the most famous figures in ancient Greek mythology. His father was Zeus, and his mother was the mortal woman Alcmene, the granddaughter of Perseus. Thus, Hercules was born a demi-god with amazing strength and stamina. Even though Hercules performed incredible feats and was considered to be a great protector and the champion of the weak, his life was far from easy. This was because Zeus' wife Hera knew that he was Zeus' illegitimate son and wanted to destroy him.

Zeus had sworn that the next born son of the Perseid house would be appointed as the king of Greece. However, due to Hera's tricks, another child, Eurystheus, was born before Hercules, and he was appointed as the king. Hercules had to serve Eurystheus when he grew up and also suffer Hera's vengeful persecution. His first exploit came about when Hera sent serpents to poison and kill him while he was still in his cradle; however, Hercules strangled both the serpents.

Hercules was brought up in the court of Amphitryon, where the best tutors in the land taught him how to sing, play the lyre, how to drive the chariot, archery, fencing, horseback riding, and wrestling. Hercules, however, not knowing his strength accidentally killed Linus, his music teacher, by hitting him with a lyre. In order to keep him out of trouble, he was then sent to herd flocks. While tending flocks, he had heard that a band of Minyans had defeated the Theban army. Thinking that it was unjust, he set off to defeat the Minyans and restore order in Thebes. As a sign of gratitude, Thebes, the King of Creon, gave him his daughter Megara in marriage. He went on to have three sons with Megara.

Hera, however, could not tolerate this situation. So, she sent a madness upon Hercules, which made him kill his wife and three young children. When he came to his senses, he was overcome with grief. In order to atone for his sins, he was obliged to serve Eurystheus. Eurystheus imposed the famous Labors upon Hercules, which were later arranged in a cycle of twelve. The 12 Labors of Hercules were:

1. The slaying of the Nemean Lion who was not affected by any weapons. Hercules strangled the lion with his bare hands and wore its skin thereafter.

2. Killing the 9-headed monster of Lerna known as Hydra.

3. Capturing the elusive Cerynitian Hind (or stag) of Arcadia, who was sacred to the goddess Artemis.

4. Capturing the wild boar of Mount Erymanthus.

5. Cleaning the cattle stables of King Augeas of Elis in a single day.

6. Driving away the monstrous man-eating birds of the Stymphalian marshes. Hercules killed them by shooting them with his arrows when they were in flight.

7. Capturing and bringing back the mad Cretan Bull that was terrorizing the island of Crete.

8. Bringing back the Mares of the Thracian King Diomedes, who used to feed human flesh to his horses. Hercules killed Diomedes and fed his flesh to the horses and then brought them back to Eurystheus.

9. Bringing back the girdle of Hippolyte, who was the queen of the Amazons. Her girdle symbolized her right to rule.

10. Seizing of the cattle of the king of Cadiz, Geryon, who ruled the island Erytheia in the far west.

11. Retrieving the Golden Apples of Hesperides, which were kept at the world's end.

12. Capturing Cerberus, the triple-headed guard dog of the underworld. Hercules wrestled Cerberus into submission and took him to Eurystheus, who was so scared of the dog that he told Hercules that his labors were complete, and that he could take Cerberus back to the gates of the underworld.

Jason

Jason, the Pan-Hellenic mythological hero, was known for his adventures with the Argonauts in search of the Golden Fleece in the Black Sea. It became one of the most enduring and popular legends in Greek mythology. He was the son of Alcimede and

Aeson, and was supposed to succeed his father as the King of Iolkos. However, his half-uncle Pelias usurped the position. He was sent away to the Centaur Chiron for his own safety by his father Aeson. It was believed that the wise Chiron taught Jason in the forests of Mount Pelion.

When Jason reached the age of twenty, he returned to Iolkos to take his kingdom back. On his way to Iolkos, while trying to help a disguised Hera cross the river Anaurus, he lost one of his sandals in the river. Hera hated Pelias because he had neglected to honor her. It was believed that Hera had secretly blessed Jason at this point and turned him into a weapon through which she could bring about Pelias' death in the future. When Jason entered the city, Pelias came to know him as the man with one sandal and recalled an oracle which had said that Pelias would die at the hands of a one-sandaled man. Jason introduced himself as the son of Aeson and the rightful King of Iolkos. Pelias, in fear of Jason, sent him on an impossibly hard adventure to retrieve the Golden Fleece and bring it to Iolkos. He promised him that he would step down from the throne if he is successful in his quest.

Accepting the quest gladly, Jason built a boat and assembled a group of heroes, which were collectively known as the Argonauts. They were named so after the Jason's ship, Argo. Jason and the Argonauts met with several perils and adventures in the course of their journey to bring the Golden

Fleece from the island of Colchis to Iolkos, and overcame all of them.

When they finally reached Colchis, they were welcomed by King Aeetes. The King had the Golden Fleece in his possession after it had been gifted to him by Phrixus. Aeetes promised to give it to Jason if he could finish some seemingly impossible tasks within a single day. Jason was left in utter desperation after being given this challenge. However, his guardian-goddess Hera persuaded Aphrodite to make Eros shoot his arrows and hit Aeetes' daughter Medea so that she would fall in love with Jason. Apart from being a princess, Medea was also a high priestess who was well-versed in magic and sorcery. With Medea's help, Jason completed all the tasks given by Aeetes. Even after Jason completed the tasks successfully, Aeetes didn't want to hand over the Golden Fleece to him. Instead, he plotted to kill Jason and the Argonauts during the night. However, Medea showed the location of the Golden Fleece to Jason and also helped him take it.

After returning to Iolkos with the Golden Fleece, Pelias refused to give up his throne. Medea then made another magic potion and convinced Pelias' daughters that Pelias could gain everlasting youth if they cut him up in pieces and boiled him in the potion. They did it and thus killed Pelias. However, Jason didn't take the throne, and instead made Akastos, Pelias' son, the ruler. He then married Medea and together they left to settle in Corinth.

Hector

The story of Hector mainly comes from the *Iliad* (written by Homer), which was one of the two complete works from the Epic Cycle.

According to Greek legend, Hector was the eldest son of Priam, the King of Troy, and his queen Hecuba. Troy prospered under Priam, and his family line seemed secured. Hector was supposed to grow up in Troy as the heir to Priam. However, fate intervened to make sure that prince Hector would never become the King of Troy.

In Troy, Hector was married to the Cilician princess Andromache, who subsequently became one of the most famous Trojan women. Hector also had a son called Astyanax with her. Andromache is universally described as the perfect wife who supported her husband and was the perfect future queen of Troy. In spite of this though, she would often plead with her husband to not leave the safety of Troy and take part in the battles that were raging outside the city walls. Hector, however, would always put his duty to protect Troy above his duties as a husband, and continued fighting on even though he recognized the inevitability of defeat. It was because of his piety, sense of courage, and his duty towards his city that Hector was such an important figure in ancient Greek history.

When the Achaean forces arrived at Troy, Hector severely reprimanded his brother Paris for bringing Helen, which could bring destruction to their home. He also belittled Paris when he declined to fight Menelaus in single combat, which could have potentially avoided the full-scale war from taking place. In spite of everything, the duty-bound Hector lead the Trojan forces against the invading Achaean troops. Hector is credited with the killing of Protesilaus, the first Achaean hero who set foot on the beaches outside Troy. Despite the efforts of Hector and Cycnus, the Achaean army gained a foothold on the beaches, and thus the 10-year war began.

Hector lead from the forefront throughout the war. His chief exploits included his fight with Ajax, the son of Telamon, his defense of the wounded Sarpedon, and the storming of the Greek ramparts. He died after a series of events involving Patroclus and Achilles. Achilles had deserted the Greeks after an argument with Agamemnon, and Hector had managed to drive them back to their ships and almost succeeded in lighting them on fire. He also slayed Patroclus with Apollo's help. Patroclus had come disguised as Achilles to help the Greeks. After his death, Achilles was devastated and returned to war, wanting to avenge his friend's death. Upon his return to the battlefield, Achilles killed Hector. With the death of Hector, Troy not only lost its greatest defender but also its last hope.

Achilles was still angry and so he dragged Hector's body behind his chariot around Patroclus' tomb and the camp. However, Apollo and Aphrodite preserved his body from mutilation and corruption. After some time, Priam and Hermes visited Achilles and begged him to return Hector's body, and thus, Hector returned to Troy one last time.

Odysseus

Odysseus is one of the most popular characters in Greek mythology and literature. He was the main hero in *Odyssey*, an epic poem by Homer. According to Homer, he was born to Laertes and Anticleia. He later became the king of Ithaca, married Penelope and had a son, Telemachus with her.

Odysseus was described by Homer as a man having excellent endurance, courage, eloquence, resourcefulness, wisdom, and shrewdness. The *Iliad* describes him as a hero who was easily able to deal with the difficulties in private relationships between the Greeks. He also played an important part in reuniting Achilles and Agamemnon. His skills and bravery in fighting were repeatedly demonstrated, and his night expedition with Diomedes against the Trojan army notably showed his courage.

The main theme of the *Odyssey* revolves around Odysseus' travels and how he regained his house and his territory. It also describes how he used a wooden horse to bring about the surrender of Troy. Among the 24 books in the epic *Odyssey*, books VI to XIII talk about his travels between Ithaca and Troy, and the challenges he faced along the way.

In the *Odyssey*, Odysseus has several chances to use his skills to be deceptive and unfair; however, he constantly chooses to be courageous, and demonstrate his loyalty, and courage. Classical Greek writers often described him as a wise and honorable statesman and sometimes as an unscrupulous politician. Philosophers generally admired his wisdom and intelligence.

Prometheus

In Greek mythology, Prometheus was a Titan who was considered to be the god of fire and had a reputation of being a clever trickster. The apparent meaning of his name is Forethinker, which emphasizes his intellectual side. As per Hesiod's *Theogony*, Prometheus was the son of Iapetus and Clymene, and his brothers were fellow Titans Atlas, Menoetius, and Epimetheus. He had a son with his Pyrrha, who was named Deucalion and was an equivalent of Noah.

In a few myths, the first human was created by Prometheus using clay. However, according to other myths, everything on earth was created by the gods, and they gave Prometheus and Epimetheus the duty of giving them gifts so that everyone could live and thrive. Epimetheus liberally gave away his offerings like wings and fur; however, he had run out of gifts by the time he came around to humans.

Prometheus felt sorry for man's naked and weak state, and so he raided Athena and Hephaistos' workshop on Mount Olympus and ran off with fire. He placed it in an empty fennel-stalk and gave it to mankind so that they could overcome their struggles in life. He even trained men how to make use of the fire. In another version of the myth, man already had fire, but Zeus took it away in anger when Prometheus tried to deceive him. Prometheus then stole the fire and gave it back to the humans.

Zeus was outraged when Prometheus stole fire and gave it to the humans, and so he punished him by taking to the Caucasus. There, Zeus chained him to a pillar where an eagle would come every day and consume Prometheus' liver. His liver grew back each night, and so the eagle came back every day to torture him endlessly. Only after several years was Prometheus freed of this punishment when the hero Hercules shot one of his poisoned arrows and killed the eagle, while passing by during his celebrated labors.

According to Hesiod's *Work & Days*, Zeus penalized mankind for accepting the fire from Prometheus. In retaliation, he commanded Hephaistos to create the first woman, who was named Pandora. All the negative aspects of life like illness, toil, war, and death would strike mankind through her, and this would forever divide mankind and the gods. Zeus sent Pandora down to Epimetheus, who married her despite Prometheus' warnings. As a wedding gift, Zeus gave Pandora a box filled with all the evils in the world. Pandora opened the box, and unleashed disease, toil, and evils that would forever plague humanity. This is where the modern day saying 'Pandora's Box' originates from.

Orpheus

In Greek mythology, Orpheus is popular for his skills in playing the lyre. He had an amazing musical pedigree as he was taught in the art of music by the god Apollo, who was considered to be one of the finest musicians, and his mother was the Muse Calliope (the patron of epic poetry). His father was Oeagrus, the King of the kingdom of Thrace.

Orpheus had gone to Egypt, but then returned to Greece to become a member of Jason's quest to search for the Golden Fleece located on the Black Sea in Colchis. The amazing musician played his gentle notes to keep the Argonauts as well as the rowers of the ship entertained. He also helped end drunken brawls among the mariners. According to myths, Orpheus' seductive singing even calmed the seas and charmed the horrible Sirens who used to tempt sailors to their deaths.

On his return, he was married to Eurydice. Their happiness was, however, short-lived as Eurydice was soon killed when she was bitten by a poisonous snake. Distraught, Orpheus ventured down to the Greek Underworld in an attempt to bring Eurydice back to life. He used his music to charm Charon, the ferryman, and the fearsome hound Cerberus to allow him to enter the land of the dead. Hades, the king of the underworld, was moved by his music and grief and subsequently allowed him to take his love back to the world of life and light. However, Hades set one condition. Eurydice would follow Orpheus as he left Hades, but she would remain in the underworld if he looked back even once during their journey home. Orpheus was delighted with this offer, and the couple walked through the shadows of Hades. Orpheus, however, was consumed with doubt and turned around to see if Eurydice was really following him. As soon as he looked around and saw her, she disappeared. Consumed with hopelessness, he collapsed after stumbling into the daylight. He refused to be in the presence of humans and didn't sing or play music again.

Orpheus was later killed by the women of Thrace. The reason and method of his death differ in different versions of the myth. The earliest known story that Orpheus was torn into pieces after he preached that Dionysos was not the greatest god. It was said that Orpheus' head, still whispering his lover's name, had been deposited on the shores of Lesbos by the tides. The dismembered limbs of Orpheus were gathered up and buried by the Muses, and his lyre was placed in the sky in the form of a constellation.

Aeneas

A mythical hero of Rome and Troy, Aeneas was the son of Anchises and the goddess Aphrodite. He was considered a Trojan hero in Greek mythology. To punish Aphrodite, Zeus made her fall in love with the herdsman, Anchises. The herdsman was smitten by her beauty. Aphrodite revealed her true identity after sleeping with him and reassured him that there would be no consequences if he kept it a secret. She then gave birth to Aeneas.

Aeneas was Hector's cousin and a member of the royal line of Troy. Aeneas played a crucial part in protecting the city of Troy against the Greek troops during the Trojan War. He was second only to Hector in ability. According to Homer, Aeneas despised his subordinate position, and because of this, a story emerged later that Aeneas might have aided the Greeks and betrayed Troy. However, a more popular version of the myth suggests that Aeneas was in fact the leader of the Trojan survivors after the Greeks took over Troy.

Chapter 5: Monsters in Greek Mythology

One of the most famous aspects of Greek mythology is its heroes. But what makes someone a hero? It's mostly having monsters to fight that makes someone a hero, and luckily for the heroes of ancient Greece, there were many terrifying and strange monsters to overcome. Greek mythology had a wide range of monsters, including Demons, Giants, Dragons, Ghosts as well as multi-formed creatures like Chimera, Manticores, Centaurs, Minotaur, and Sphinx.

Typhon

Typhon is one of the most fearsome deities in Greek mythology, as he is simultaneously both a god and a monster. He was an extremely tall giant whose head could touch the stars. He had the torso of a man; however, his legs were made up of coils of vipers that would attack others as he moved. His main head had about a hundred dragons' heads on it, which would produce different animal sounds. He had glowing red eyes, which would terrify anyone who looked into them. He also had a savage jaw that could breathe fire. His hands were made up of hundreds of snake coils similar to his legs that could stretch from east to west. He also had wings, pointed ears, and a filthy, matted beard.

Typhon was the last son of Tartarus (of the nether world) and Gaia (Earth). According to some stories, Hera wanted to create a god who was stronger than Zeus and thus, made the two gods give birth to Typhon. Typhon was the father of all monsters. He was considered similar to a 100-headed fire-breathing dragon that never slept. His wife was Echidna, who was believed to be the mother of all monsters. The two of them had several children, including the Chimera, the multi-headed Lernaean Hydra, and Cerberus, the 3-headed hound of Hades.

Typhon had numerous battles with Zeus. According to one story, in his rage, Typhon had destroyed several cities and even thrown mountains. Because of this, most of the Olympian gods were scared of him and transformed into their animal forms to hide. Only Zeus, Athena, and Dionysus remained in their original forms. When Athena called Zeus a coward, it spurred him to attack Typhon before capturing Mount Olympus. Zeus cornered Typhon by striking hundreds of lightning bolts at him. After defeating Typhon, the god cast him into the bottomless pit of Tartarus. Zeus then put an entire mountain over the pit to prevent Typhon from ever coming out. The mountain was known as Mount Etna.

The ancient Greeks believed volcanic eruptions were caused by Typhon trying to escape, as he was a fearsome fire-breathing monster. It was also believed that earthquakes were caused by the movements of Typhon trying to flee.

Sphinx

The Sphinx is a mythological creature having the body of a lion, and a human head. In some versions, the Sphinx is depicted as having wings. It is an important image in both Greek and Egyptian art and legend. In ancient Greek culture, the Sphinx had a head of a woman, while in Egyptian versions, the creature had a male head – either animal or human. The Sphinx can also be seen in the sculptures and arts of the Phoenician, Persian, Assyrian, and Mycenaean civilizations.

The views of the ancient Greeks were different from that of the Egyptians. They saw the Sphinx as a troublesome creature. One of the most popular myths involving a sphinx is that of the Theban prince Oedipus. According to Hesiod's Theogony, Thebes' territory in Greece was being terrorized by a sphinx that was born from the fire-breathing monster Chimera. This Sphinx was said to be the sister of the Nemean lion and the half-sister of the three-headed dog Kerberos. The Sphinx brought famine and drought and would leave Thebes' territory only if they could solve her riddle.

The riddle was as follows: "What walks on four feet in the morning, two in the afternoon, and three at night?"

The Sphinx killed and ate anyone who dared to answer the riddle incorrectly. The Sphinx also killed Thebes' son Haimon, and then the king of Kreon became so desperate that he offered his daughter Iokaste as well as his kingdom to anyone who could correctly answer the riddle. The challenge was taken up by Oedipus, and he gave the correct answer, which was man. As an infant, man walks on all fours. In adulthood, he walks on two feet. In old age, he walks with a cane.

In ancient Greek art and culture, sphinxes first appeared in sculptures during the seventh century BCE. They were made using clay and were generally linked with Crete, where the molded heads of sphinxes were commonplace. These sculptures were generally kept on top of tall Doric or Ionic columns. They were also kept at sanctuary sites like Olympia and Delphi.

Cyclops

In ancient Greek mythology, a Cyclops is a gigantic, one-eyed monster with enormous strength. According to the Greeks, an entire race of Cyclopes lived on an island without law and order. In the Iliad, Homer portrays the Cyclopes as savage but pastoral, which was typical of the strange creatures that were invented by the Greeks.

In Theogony, Hesiod wrote that the Cyclopes were the children of Sky (Uranus) and Earth (Gaia), which made them the generation before the Olympian Gods. They were thought to live in a faraway land whose name and location were unknown.

They had a simple pastoral life living in caves and herding goats and sheep. Originally, there were 3 Cyclopes, and Hesiod named them Arges (Bright), Steropes (Lightning), and Brontes (Thunder). These three Cyclopes would go on to father more of their kind. However, Apollo later killed the trio. It was believed that the ghosts of the original Cyclopes haunted Mount Etna volcano in Sicily.

Hesiod also said that the Cyclopes had 'very violent hearts,' which made them similar to other fantastic creatures in Greek mythology like the centaurs, which represented lawlessness. Living in isolation, they had insular and solitary lives. They had no society, government, or sense of community. Civilized Greeks considered these deficiencies to be abominable.

The Cyclopes helped Zeus and the other Olympian gods in their 10-year battle known as the Titanomachy, to defeat the Titans and gain control of the universe. Uranus had imprisoned the Cyclopes because of their unruly behavior. After their release, they made thunderbolts for Zeus as a sign of their gratitude. Zeus used the thunderbolts as a weapon to strike down and kill his enemies. The Cyclopes also created a helmet for Hades, which could make the wearer invisible, the silver bow for Artemis, and Poseidon's trident. They also excelled in building walls, including the large Mycenaean fortification walls, which used large and irregular shaped blocks. The acropolis of Tiryns and Mycenae still have long stretches of Cyclopean walls even today. Thus, in modern archeology, the term Cyclopean is used to describe walls in which the stones are not rounded.

One of the most famous encounters between a Cyclops and a human was endured by the hero Odysseus on his way back from the Trojan War. Homer's Odyssey recounts the remarkable story where Odysseus and his companions became trapped in the cave of Polyphemus upon landing on the island of the Cyclopes, and details how they escaped death by blinding the Cyclops.

Chimera

Chimera is one of the most popular and frightening monsters to appear in the stories of Greek mythology. A fire-breathing hybrid monster, Chimera is mentioned in several works, including Homer's Iliad, and Hesiod's Theogony, amongst others. The ancient sources describe her as a monster having the body of a lion and two heads protruding from her body. One of the heads was of a she-goat and the other a lion from which she breathed a stream of fire. In addition to that, she had a snake as a tail. The ferocious Chimera had several animal attributes in many respects. She embodied the intelligence of a goat, the strength of a lion, and a snake's cunningness.

It was believed that Chimera was the offspring of 2 of the most famous monsters of Greek mythology, Typhon and Echidna.

Chimera had several famous siblings, including Cerberus, the Lernaean Hydra, Orthus, and the Colchian Dragon. According to Hesiod's genealogy of the gods, it was believed that Chimera was female and would mate with Orthus to give birth to 2 more monsters, the Sphinx and the Nemean Lion.

Chimera was mostly associated with the region of Lycia in Asia Minor. It was thought that King Amisodarus raised her to maturity; however, she was released into the Lycian countryside after becoming too dangerous. Chimera would then terrorize the region of Lycia and kill the unwary. She would generally appear in front of Greek sailors immediately before any grave misfortune. If someone saw her, usually a volcanic eruption, a terrible storm, or a shipwreck would follow.

The King Iobates of Lycia eventually bested Chimera with the help of Bellerophon. The Corinthian hero, Bellerophon, had been staying as a guest of King Proetus (Iobates' son-in-law). King Iobates sent Bellerophon on the seemingly impossible quest to kill the monster Chimera.

No one had succeeded in killing Chimera, largely due to the dangers of her fire-laden breath. However, Bellerophon had an important ally in the form of the Greek goddess Athena, who sent him the flying horse Pegasus. Bellerophon climbed on top of Pegasus and flew above Chimera's head. He added a chunk of lead at the end of his spear, and when Chimera breathed fire trying to incinerate him, he threw the spear into her throat. The melting lead suffocated and killed Chimera.

Empusa

In Greek mythology, Empusa was the beautiful daughter of the spirit Mormo and the goddess Hecate. She is believed to be the first vampire-like monster in Greek mythology. However, even before Empusa made her first appearance in western mythology, similar creatures were also found in eastern traditions like the Hindu and Chinese mythology.

According to Greek mythology, Empusa seduced young men and feasted on their blood. The young men she seduced would fall into a deep sleep after their climax, and she would then drink their blood and feast on their flesh. In human form, Empusa was described as an irresistibly beautiful young woman with flaming hair, a leg of bronze, and the hoofed foot of a horse. She was always seen wearing brazen sandals.

According to Roman mythology, Empusa had stopped being a demigoddess and became a wandering specter-like being, or a group of beings. A group of Empusa known as Empusae, used to devour unsuspecting travelers. They would leave their bones at crossroads to scare the unwary travelers. They were said to have shape-shifting abilities and thought to have preferred the shape of a young woman to attack, and the shape of an owl or Strix to move faster at night.

Philostratus, a Greek philosopher of the Roman Imperial period, said that the best method of protecting yourself from the attack of the Empusae was to hurl insults at them. It was believed that at the sound of foul language, the Empusae used to run and hide while uttering a high-pitched scream.

The Empusae are most popularly known for their appearance in *The Frogs* by Aristophanes, in which they frightened Xanthias and Dionysus while they were on their way to the underworld. However, with time, the term 'Empusae' became a general term representing nocturnal demons linked with sleep. As the Empusae fed on their victims while they were asleep, they were attributed with creating the phenomenon of sleep paralysis. In the medieval times, they were linked with the Succubus, who were depraved entities that used to prey on innocent men while they were sleeping.

Hydra

In Greek legend, Hydra, also known as the Lernaean Hydra, is one of the most iconic monsters. According to Hesiod's *Theogony*, Hydra was the monstrous offspring of Typhon, the most powerful Greek monster, and Echidna, the mother of monsters. The Lernaean Hydra was the sibling of other notable monsters like the Colchian Dragon, Cerberus, and Chimera. However, the Lernaean Hydra was not raised by Echidna, as the goddess Hera took the monster into her care. She raised her for one specific purpose: the death of Zeus' illegitimate son Hercules.

In a broader sense, the Lernaean Hydra was thought to be a sea snake; however, it was not a regular size serpent as it was huge in size. It is famous for its numerous heads, and while it was often said that it had about fifty heads, more common depictions show that it had just nine heads, one of which was immortal. Each of these heads was also said to exhale poisonous gases.

The Hydra resided in Lerna, and hence the name Lernaean was given to the monster. Lerna was a region situated on the east coast of Peloponnese on the south of Argos. Lerna was noted particularly for its swamps, springs, and lakes, which were all gifts from Poseidon, and also for the purity and healing properties of the freshwater found in the region. Another important aspect of the region was the fact that it was also the home to one of the doors to the Underworld. The Hydra's titular role was to guard this door to the Underworld, and the monster would kill any unwary travelers. However, Hydra's presence in the waterways made the bountiful freshwater undrinkable.

The Lernaean Hydra gained popularity because of the Greek hero Hercules, who was given the seemingly impossible task of killing the Hydra. Hercules traveled to Lerna and eventually found the Lernaean Hydra in one of its lairs. As it charged towards Hercules, he took up his sword and decapitated a head of the Hydra with a single swipe. However, the Hydra grew two new, fully formed heads from the open neck wound.

Hercules then took the help of his nephew, Iolaus, and came up with the plan to cauterize the open cuts before a new pair of heads could emerge from it. Thus, as Hercules decapitated a head, Iolaus cauterized the wound with a flaming torch. Eventually, only the one immortal head of the Hydra remained. Hera had been watching the encounter between Hercules and her monster and sent a second monster, which was a gigantic crab called Carcinus, to assist the Lernaean Hydra. However, Hercules simply crushed the crab and destroyed the Hydra's final head with a golden sword given to him by Athena.

After the Hydra's death, Hera turned both the monsters into constellations. Carcinus became the constellation Cancer, while the Hydra became a constellation known simply as Hydra.

Cerberus

According to Greek mythology, Cerberus was a watchdog of the Underworld. As the Hound of Hades, he is one of the most easily recognized monsters of Greek mythology. Cerberus was also the offspring of Typhon and Echidna. The most prominent feature of the monster was the presence of 3 dog heads on a single body. Cerberus was a genuinely deadly beast with other features like the claws of a lion, the tail of a serpent, and a mane made of snakes.

The Underworld, the domain of Hades, was Cerberus' home. The primary job of the giant hound was to guard the Underworld. This meant that Cerberus' role was to guard the Gates of Hell from any unwanted visitors. It would also patrol the Acheron River banks to stop the shadows of the dead from escaping. However, there were also success stories of mortals entering the Underworld, including the likes of Orpheus, Pirithous, and Theseus, who all made it past the gigantic Hound of Hades.

Cerberus would ultimately gain his popularity because of his fight with the great Greek hero, Hercules. Hercules' 12th and final labor was to bring back Cerberus from the gates of the Underworld. The fearless hero descended into the Underworld and made Charon take him across the Acheron River. However, instead of simply capturing Cerberus and risking Hades' anger, Hercules went to the god's palace and talked to Hades and his wife, Persephone. Hercules asked for them to allow him to take Cerberus from the Underworld. Hades granted his permission on the condition that his hound would not be harmed in any way and would be returned to the Underworld once the labor was done.

Hercules went about his labor of subduing Cerberus. Keeping his weapons on one side, the great hero wrestled the gigantic hound and trapped the monster in a chokehold. After wrestling Cerberus into submission, Hercules then dragged the 3-headed monster out of the Underworld. Hercules led Cerberus through Greece to the court of King Eurystheus, and all the people who saw the great Hound of Hades were extremely scared. With this, Hercules finished his final labor and returned Cerberus back to the Underworld. After that, the monstrous dog would watch over the shadows of the deceased once again.

Minotaur

In Greek mythology, the Minotaur was a popular and recognizable monster of Crete that was part man and part bull. Minotaur's story started on the island of Crete during the reign of King Minos, who was the son of the God Zeus and Europa. When Asterius, the King of Crete, died, Minos prayed to the Greek god Poseidon to send him a bull from the sea. He promised that he would sacrifice the bull to him afterward. Poseidon responded to his prayer, and Minos was crowned the King of Crete.

However, the magnificently white, mighty, and virile bull was so beautiful that Minos decided to sacrifice another bull in its place. Poseidon was extremely angered by this act and made Minos' wife, Pasiphae fall in love with the Cretan Bull. Pasiphae was incapable of resisting her lust and persuaded Daedalus to make her a hollowed wooden cow. She hid inside it until the Cretan Bull mated with her. As a result of this unnatural union, the Minotaur was born.

Needless to say, Minos was horrified by the sight of the Minotaur, and to cover up his disgrace, he ordered Daedalus to construct a structure so complex that it would be not only impossible for the monster to leave but also hard for anyone going in to make their way out. Daedalus made the plan to construct a huge underground maze of passages and hallways that came to be known as the Labyrinth.

The Labyrinth's center became the dark dwelling place of the Minotaur. The monster was regularly fed human flesh there, particularly that of 14 young noble Athenian boys and girls. The city of Athens sent them on a yearly basis as a sacrifice in order to recompense for the death of Androgeus, who was Minos' son.

However, the great hero Theseus of Athens could not turn a blind eye to his fellow citizens' sufferings. Thus, he volunteered to go to Crete when the time for the third sacrifice arrived. Lucky for him, Minos' daughter Ariadne fell in love with him and helped him. She persuaded Daedalus to tell her the secret behind the Labyrinth. At his advice, she gave a ball of thread to Theseus, and the hero used it to navigate his way through the Labyrinth. At last, Theseus came across the Minotaur at the center of the Labyrinth. After a long and tiring fight, Theseus was finally able to defeat the vicious monster.

Medusa

Medusa is arguably one of the most famous villainous monsters of Greek mythology. In Theogony, Hesiod wrote that there were three gorgons – Medusa, Stheno, and Euryale, who were the monstrous offspring of Ceto and Phorcys. Ceto and Phorcys were also parents to other monsters, including Graeae, Ladon, and Echidna. A few ancient stories also tell the tale of how Ceto had given birth to the Gorgons in one of the caves situated deep below Mount Olympus.

Medusa and her sisters were traditionally described as winged women with huge heads. Their heads had large staring eyes and the tusks of a swine. In addition to that, the Gorgons were also believed to have brass hands. The hairs on their heads were the most striking feature of the sisters as each strand was made of a hissing snake. However, Medusa was not considered the deadliest of the 3 Gorgon sisters. This accolade was given to Stheno, who was said to have killed more people than both Euryale and Medusa. According to Hesiod, the Gorgons stayed on an island. This island was situated near the island of the

Hesperides in the western end of the world. However, some stories also claimed that they lived in Libya.

According to old stories, Medusa was different from her sisters, as she was mortal and was also born with a beautiful face. As a beautiful maiden, she had foolishly declared herself to be as beautiful as Athena. Medusa's beauty would attract Poseidon's attention, the sea god. Poseidon, unable to control his lustful thoughts, raped Medusa in Athena's temple. Athena could not let this act of desecration go unpunished. However, she could not punish Poseidon, and so she punished Medusa instead, by transforming her into a monster. After this incident, Medusa left her house and stayed with the Gorgons.

Medusa became famous for her part in the adventures of Perseus. In order to get rid of Perseus, King Polydectes of Seriphos tricked him into accepting a quest to bring the head of Medusa. With the help of Hermes and Athena, Perseus finally arrived at the land of the Gorgons. While Medusa was asleep, Perseus used the reflection in Athena's bronze shield and managed to cut off Medusa's head with his sickle. However, Medusa was pregnant at that time, and when Perseus cut off her head, Pegasus and Chrysaor, her two sons by Poseidon, sprung from her severed neck.

The severed head had the power of turning anyone who looked at it into stone. It was given to Athena, who kept it in her shield.

Chapter 6: Famous Greek Mythology Tales

Sisyphus

The myth of Sisyphus endures because of the torment that he endured in Tartarus, a section of the Underworld.

Sisyphus was a king and ruler who encouraged trade and established a lot of good for his city but was also known for his ruthlessness. One of the most important rules in Ancient Greece was the idea of hospitality: you were to treat your guests well. Feed them, bathe them, and help them if you could.

However, Sisyphus would kill his guests and show their bodies off to his people to remind them of his power. This blatant disregard for the sacred rules of hospitality angered Zeus. He tried to have Sisyphus killed, but was outsmarted by Sisyphus on multiple occasions. Eventually, Zeus succeeded in killing Sisyphus, and upon dying he was banished to the Underworld.

In Tartarus, Sisyphus's punishment was to push a large boulder up a hill to the top, but each time when he gets close to the top, the weight would prove too great and the rock would roll back to the bottom, and so Sisyphus would have to start all over again for eternity.

Nowadays, if someone has a "Sisyphean task," they are doing something that they will never actually get to finish.

Hyacinthus

Hyacinthus (also known as Hyacinth) was a young, handsome Spartan Prince. Hyacinthus was a great friend, and also lover of the god Apollo.

One day, whilst walking upon a hillside, Apollo saw another shepherd boy, who was playing music on a pipe. Apollo was attracted by his music and headed towards him. As Apollo drew near, he stopped and stood before the shepherd, asking " What is thy name, noble youth?". The shepherd was stunned by the brightness emanating from the god, but responded simply. " Hyacinthus".

Apollo then asked Hyacinthus if he could use his pipe to play some music of his own. Hyacinthus was amazed at the incredible beauty of Apollo but was even more awestruck by the sound of his music, as it was unlike anything a mortal had ever heard before. Hyacinthus stood and watched silently in awe. Apollo finally finished playing, and handed back the pipe, saying frankly, "I like you, Hyacinthus.' We will be friends, and you shall go with me to the palace of King Admetus."

Hyacinthus' eyes lit up; he badly wanted to go, but thinking of his duties as a shepherd, he said, " But what would become of my sheep? I must not leave them. No, no, Apollo; I cannot go with you!"

Instead, Apollo decided that he would visit Hyacinthus the following day. True to his word, Apollo returned again; and for many long days they played, talked, and learned to love one another.

Their relationship was beautiful, and they continue to spend most of their time together. Unfortunately, that all ended on one fateful day when they were playing a game of discus. Hyacinthus wished that Apollo would win the game, and Apollo wished for the success of Hyacinthus.

Apollo picked up the discus and performed a powerful throw. He would have won, but The West Wind intervened. The West Wind had grown jealous of their beautiful friendship. Thinking that his actions would make them quarrel, he changed the direction of the wind. The discus was blown so forcefully that it bounded back and hit Hyacinthus on the forehead, knocking him to the ground.

Hyacinthus took a mighty blow to the head, taking both him and Apollo by surprise. Apollo rushed toward his friend and lifted his wounded head from the ground. Hyacinthus however was unresponsive, and his head drooped like a broken flower. Hyacinthus had died instantly from the impact. Apollo had instantly lost his beloved friend in such a cruel and unpredictable way.

Where the blood of Hyacinthus had fallen, Apollo caused a flower to spring up from the ground. This is of course the Hyacinth flower that we know of today.

Procne and Philomena

Pandion, the King of Athens, married his maternal Aunt, Zeuxippe. Together, they had two daughters, Procne and Philomela, and also twin sons, Erechtheus and Butes. Pandion, however, wasn't a great father, and was constantly preoccupied with his kingdom. When Athens went to war with Abdacus, Pandion called upon his neighbor Tereus who resided in Thrace, and asked for his help.

Tereus was not only the ruler of Daulis, but was also the son of Ares. Thanks to his many connections in Thrace, he won the war for Pandion. Pandion, being a diplomat and smart businessman, decided that Tereus should be well rewarded. He also aimed to consolidate a relationship with him, and since he was a horrible father who saw his daughters primarily as bargaining tools, gave his daughter Procne to Tereus to be his wife.

Tereus had his way with Procne, and then left her alone to take care of their son, Itys. After she was impregnated however, Tereus abandoned Procne in his house out in the country, telling nobody of her whereabouts. Then, he went to the home of Pandion, with his eyes set on Philomela. He lied to Philomela, telling her that her sister had died. He proceeded to seduce Philomela, and soon thereafter, they were married.

Upon marrying her, Tereus cut Philomena's tongue out. Philomela, however, was an accomplished weaver, and she wove characters into a robe in order to communicate to her sister. Once she realized that Procne was in fact alive, she sent the robe to Procne so that she could know what had happened. Procne immediately set out to get her revenge, bringing her son, Itys, with her.

Procne pretended to play along with Tereus' evil ways and told him that she would make him a magnificent dinner. She then went into the kitchen, where she killed their son Itys. She proceeded to boil him and served him to Tereus. While Tereus unknowingly feasted on his own son, Procne grabbed Philomela and ran.

Once Tereus realized that the sisters had disappeared, he took an axe and went after them. The women ran, but they were not making much ground. They prayed to the Gods to be turned into birds, and the Gods took pity upon them. Procne was transformed into the nightingale, constantly crying her sorrow in the sounds, "Itu, Itu" (the name of her son). Philomela became the voiceless swallow. Tereus was also changed into a bird, and became the hoopoe, which calls out, "pou, pou" which means "where, where" in Greek.

The Love Story of Eros and Psyche

The myth surrounding Eros and Psyche might be one of the best love stories in ancient Greek mythology. Eros (Cupid in Latin) was the son of Aphrodite and was considered to be the epitome of intense love and desire. He was portrayed as a man shooting arrows into the hearts of people, making them fall in love. Psyche (meaning 'soul' in Greek) was a beautiful maiden who was thought to symbolize the human soul.

Psyche was one of three daughters of a king in a Grecian kingdom. Of the three sisters, Psyche was the youngest and most beautiful. She was like a goddess among mere mortals. She had become widely popular across the entire kingdom because of her beauty, and men constantly visited the palace to worship and admire her. People used to say that she was even more beautiful than the goddess Aphrodite. All the honors that were meant for Aphrodite were showered on the simple, mortal girl.

Aphrodite was jealous of Psyche's beauty and could not accept such a situation. Therefore, she asked for her son, Eros' help, and told him to use his powers to put a spell on her. Always obedient, Eros went to her palace with two vials of potions. While Psyche was sleeping, an invisible Eros sprinkled a potion on her, making men steer clear of her when it came to marriage. However, he pricked her with one of his arrows by accident, and she woke up. Eros, in turn, was so amazed by her beauty that he pricked himself as well. Feeling ashamed of his actions, he sprinkled the other potion on her, which gave her all the joys of life.

As a result, Psyche could not find a husband even though she was still as beautiful as ever. This caused great distress and anxiety to her parents, and so they asked the oracle of Delphi for Apollo's advice regarding finding Psyche a husband. Apollo ordered Psyche to come to the summit of a mountain in a black dress and stay there alone. A winged serpent would travel there and marry her.

Succumbing to her fate, she headed to the mountain. Psyche remained seated and waited on the hill and in the dark. While she was crying in the silent night, she felt a slight breeze, the mildest of winds, which lifted her in the air, over the mountains, and into a meadow filled with flowers. When she opened her eyes, she saw an imposing and magnificent castle with floors inlaid with precious stones, silver walls, and gold columns. Her new husband proved to be a true and gentle lover. However, he never permitted her to see him. He was, of course, Eros himself. Even without seeing him, Psyche was sure that he was the loving husband she had always desired, and not a monster.

The next few days passed very joyfully, and she was extremely happy. However, she was also feeling very sad that she could not see her husband. In addition to that, she was incredibly bored as she was left alone all day. She also missed her family terribly and asked her husband to allow her sisters to visit her. When they came to visit and saw her beautiful house, they grew jealous and curious to know who her husband was. In total jealousy, they devised a plan to hurt Psyche. They told her that she shouldn't forget that the oracle had said that her husband would be a monster and that there was no doubt that he was preparing to devour her. They recommended her to keep a knife and a candle by her bed so that she could reveal his face the next time he visited her.

From that day on, Psyche couldn't think of anything else. So, the next time her husband came to visit her, she hid a knife and a candle beside her bed. When her husband was sleeping peacefully, she gathered her courage and approached the bed with a lit candle. The light showed that her husband was not a monster but was actually Eros himself. She felt relieved and thanked the gods. However, a drop of oil fell on his face while she was leaning on him, and he woke up in pain. When he saw Psyche's distrust, he left the palace without another word.

She immediately went after her husband, but she fell on the ground and lost consciousness. When she woke up, she found herself not in the palace, but instead in a field close to her old home. Not knowing what else she could do, she went to the temple of Aphrodite and asked for her help. She prayed to her to speak to Eros and persuade him to return to her. However, Aphrodite still wanted her revenge and gave her three tasks that Psyche needed to accomplish in order to prove her worthiness. However, she would lose Eros forever if she failed in any one of the tasks.

Her first task was to sort a huge pile of various grains into separate piles. Psyche lost hope at the sight of the pile. However, an army of ants helped her to separate and arrange the grains. Aphrodite returned the next morning and gave her another task. The next task was to fill a bottle with black waters from the River Estige, right where it flowed down from an incredible height. An eagle flying by decided to help her, carried the bottle up to the river, and filled it up with water. Aphrodite was livid as she knew Psyche could never have accomplished this task alone. Finally, she sent her to the Underworld with a box. She told her to ask Persephone to drain some of her beauty into the box. Persephone was glad to serve Aphrodite and did as she was asked. Psyche returned back to Earth cheerful. The goddess, however, got extremely angry when she received the box. She told the poor maiden that she would have to remain as her servant.

The Gods were watching all of this and, at that crucial moment, decided to intervene. Hermes, the messenger God explained all the difficulties that Psyche was going through to Eros. He was touched, and this cured the hurt of her betrayal. He left in search of Psyche and found her exhausted in Aphrodite's garden.

After that, Eros and Psyche lived together happily in their magnificent palace, which was always filled with flowers. As a wedding gift, Zeus let Psyche taste ambrosia, the drink of gods, and made her immortal.

Conclusion

Thank you for making it through to the end of this book!

Greek Mythology has endured for thousands of years, and even today is the inspiration behind many popular books, TV shows, and movies. I hope that you have enjoyed learning all about Greek mythology and the different Gods, Goddesses, Heroes, and Monsters that make its stories so entertaining!

Finally, if you enjoyed this book, please keep an eye out for other titles I have written on the topics of Celtic, Egyptian, and Norse mythology. These books are available on Amazon, as well as through other select retailers worldwide. Once again, thank you for choosing this book!

www.ingramcontent.com/pod-product-compliance
Lightning Source LLC
LaVergne TN
LVHW011735060526
838200LV00051B/3178